THE LITTLE BOOK OF
UNICORNS

UNICORNUCOPIA

THE LITTLE BOOK OF
UNICORNS

UNICORNUCOPIA

HarperCollins*Publishers*

HarperCollins*Publishers*
1 London Bridge Street
London SE1 9GF
www.harpercollins.co.uk

First published by HarperCollins*Publishers* in 2018

1 3 5 7 9 10 8 6 4 2

Copyright © HarperCollins*Publishers* 2018

ISBN: 978-0-00-829259-1

Printed and bound in Latvia

Dedicated to all those
unicorns at heart –
specifically Aimee, Elliott,
Saoirse, Annie K., Isla, Alex H.,
Katie H. 1 & Katie H. 2,
Millie, Lucy V., and Oli M.

Contents

Always be yourself,
UNLESS YOU CAN BE A
unicorn.
Then always be a
unicorn!

Introduction

*J*rom Confucius and Marco Polo to My Little Pony and Internet memes, humans have been enchanted by unicorns throughout history and across cultures. Just consider the hashtag *#unicorn*, with 7 million posts and counting! Today we believe unicorns are mythical creatures that never truly existed – but try telling that to Lancelot the Unicorn, who made his debut at New York's Madison Square Garden in 1984, or to the brave unicorns who gave up their horns for the Throne Chair of Denmark in 1662, or to the unicorns left behind playing in the rain as Noah boarded his ark, or to the 'sea unicorns', aka narwhals, or to Bambi the unicorn-deer, born in Florence, Italy, as recently as 2008 . . .

You see? For however hard we try to disprove their existence, the unicorns of legend stand even stronger, several thousand years old, drawing us back into their magic once more. In our quest to discover more about the unicorn, we have learned about the world around us, from the world view of ancient Japanese cultures to the mating rituals of the narwhal, and from prehistoric animal skeletons to Shakespearean allegory. So whether or not unicorns have existed, do exist, or might one day exist, the myth is more powerful than the reality. With its legendary gentle, noble nature, the unicorn has taught us to love, to believe, and to seek magic in the everyday. And with a little unicorn magic, sunshine can find its way through the clouds, kindness trumps cruelty, and we all finally have an excuse to eat rainbow cake.

History

ONE OF THE EARLIEST DESCRIPTIONS

of a unicorn

COMES FROM A BOOK WRITTEN
CIRCA 400 BCE CALLED

Indica.

THE BOOK'S AUTHOR, THE ANCIENT

Greek historian and doctor

CTESIAS, WORKED AT THE
PERSIAN COURT, WHERE HE HEARD
travellers' tales of
the fabulous beast.

CTESIAS IS ALSO CREDITED AS THE
FIRST PERSON TO ATTRIBUTE

magic

to a unicorn's horn

(GROUND INTO A POWDER, THE HORN
WAS THOUGHT TO BE MAGIC).

POTIONS

REMEDIES FOR ALL MALADIES

Indica

CTESIAS' UNICORN WAS DESCRIBED AS A

white horse

with a purple head
and blue eyes.

THE CREATURE'S HORN WAS WHITE
AT THE BASE, BLACK IN THE MIDDLE,
AND RED AT THE TIP.

'No creature, neither
horse or any other,
could overtake it.'

IT IS NOW BELIEVED THAT CTESIAS *was actually describing* A MISHMASH OF ANIMALS, INCLUDING

an Indian rhinoceros!

IN THE ANCIENT GREEK BESTIARY
KNOWN AS THE *PHYSIOLOGUS*,
the unicorn
WAS INCLUDED ALONGSIDE OTHER REAL AND
MYTHICAL ANIMALS AND DESCRIBED AS
strong and fierce.

MANY MEDIEVAL PAINTINGS
EXIST OF THE
**mythical hunt of
the unicorn,**
FROM CULTURES AS WIDE-RANGING
as Europe, China,
and the Middle East.

DID YOU KNOW?

DURING THE MIDDLE AGES,
chivalry
– A CODE OF RULES FOR GOOD MANNERS,
POLITE BEHAVIOUR, AND BRAVERY –
WAS VERY IMPORTANT IN EUROPEAN
SOCIETY. UNICORNS BECAME THE

ultimate symbol
*of chivalry for their
power, purity, and grace.*

'Unicorn borns'

WERE OFTEN EXTRAVAGANT GIFTS
for kings, queens, and churches,
COSTING THE EQUIVALENT OF THOUSANDS
OF DOLLARS OR POUNDS.

CUPS SUPPOSEDLY MADE OF
unicorn horn were highly prized
DURING THE MIDDLE AGES. THESE DRINKING VESSELS WERE BELIEVED TO CURE ILLNESSES AND TO PROTECT THE OWNERS FROM POISONED DRINKS. IN REALITY, THEY WERE PROBABLY MADE OF
rhinoceros or narwhal tusk.

A recipe for
**how best to
cook unicorn**
HAS EVEN BEEN DISCOVERED IN A
medieval cookbook!
THE 14TH-CENTURY COOKBOOK WAS
DISCOVERED AT THE BRITISH LIBRARY
AND EVEN INCLUDES ILLUSTRATIONS
OF THE POOR CREATURE BEING
roasted on a grill!

24

BBQ SECRETS
Volume 1

Ancient Beasts

Scotland's national animal is the

unicorn.

IT WAS FIRST ADOPTED AS THE NATIONAL ANIMAL BY KING ROBERT WAY BACK IN THE 1300S. THE UNICORN WAS BELIEVED TO BE THE

natural enemy of the lion –

ENGLAND'S NATIONAL SYMBOL. THIS MADE IT THE NATURAL CHOICE OF SYMBOL FOR SCOTLAND, DEFIANT OF ITS NEIGHBOUR.

The Lion and the Unicorn nursery rhyme

'THE LION AND THE UNICORN WERE
FIGHTING FOR THE CROWN,

THE LION BEAT THE UNICORN ALL
AROUND THE TOWN.

SOME GAVE THEM WHITE BREAD,
AND SOME GAVE THEM BROWN,

SOME GAVE THEM PLUM CAKE AND
DRUMMED THEM OUT OF TOWN.'

DID YOU KNOW?

IN 15TH-CENTURY SCOTLAND,
golden coins
WITH UNICORNS ON THE FLIPSIDE
WERE USED. FIRST ISSUED IN 1486 BY
KING JAMES III, THEY WERE SIMPLY CALLED
*'unicorns' and
'half-unicorns'.*

IT IS BELIEVED THAT

Queen Elizabeth I of England

OWNED A UNICORN TUSK, SAID TO BE

worth the price of a castle.

The 16th-century book *HISTORIAE ANIMALIUM*, WRITTEN BY SWISS NATURALIST CONRAD GESNER AND describing all of Earth's animals, INCLUDES AN ENTRY FOR THE **unicorn.**

Around 2000 BCE,
THE INDUS RIVER VALLEY CIVILIZATION
CREATED THE UNICORN SEAL.
The seals were
small stone squares
ONTO WHICH AN IMAGE (USUALLY
AN ANIMAL) WOULD BE DRAWN. IT IS
BELIEVED THEY WERE USED AS A WAY OF
identifying local traders.
THE UNICORN WAS THE MOST COMMON
ANIMAL ON THESE SEALS, WHICH CAN NOW
BE SEEN IN THE BRITISH MUSEUM, LONDON.

DID YOU KNOW?

IN RENAISSANCE VENICE,

unicorn horns

WERE SUPPOSEDLY TOSSED INTO
THE CANAL AT THE *PALAZZO DUCALE*,
OR DOGE'S PALACE, TO ENSURE
the water could never
be poisoned.

The Throne Chair of Denmark,

BUILT BETWEEN 1662 AND 1671,
WAS MADE FROM IVORY, PUREST GOLD,
AND, ACCORDING TO LEGEND,

unicorn born,

AND GUARDED BY THREE LIFE-SIZE
SILVER LIONS. TODAY, THE HORN
*is known to be
narwhal tusk.*

THE ELABORATE THRONE CAN STILL
BE SEEN IN THE CASTLE OF ROSENBORG,
IN COPENHAGEN.

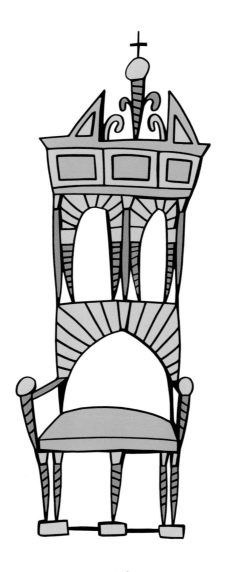

35

Myth & Magic

A unicorn's horn

IS CALLED AN

alicorn.

How are unicorns born?

NO ONE CAN ANSWER HOW THESE MYTHICAL CREATURES ARE BORN.

Do they hatch from an egg? Are they born from a female unicorn, much like a foal?

ARE THERE EVEN FEMALE UNICORNS? ALL WE DO KNOW FROM MYTHS AND RETELLINGS IS THAT UNICORNS ARE SOLITARY CREATURES AND CAN LIVE

for hundreds of years.

Were unicorns on Noah's Ark?

RELIGIOUS SCHOLARS HAVE STRUGGLED WITH THIS QUESTION. WHILE UNICORNS ARE MENTIONED IN SOME VERSIONS OF THE BIBLE, IT IS WIDELY BELIEVED THAT THIS IS BECAUSE OF A

bad translation of 'wild ox'.

GOD IS ALSO SAID TO HAVE
INSTRUCTED NOAH TO TAKE ONE MALE
AND ONE FEMALE OF EACH SPECIES IN
ORDER TO REPOPULATE THE EARTH
after the Flood.
ONE POSSIBILITY IS THAT UNICORNS
DIDN'T MAKE THE CUT, AS UNICORNS ARE
TRADITIONALLY BELIEVED TO BE MALE.
*Or perhaps they simply
missed the boat,*
AS SHEL SILVERSTEIN'S SONG
'THE UNICORN' WOULD SUGGEST!

EARLY ILLUSTRATIONS of UNICORNS WERE
# of large animals
WITH SINGLE HOOVES AND BLACK
HORNS. SOME SHOWED THEM AS LARGE
RHINOCEROS-LIKE CREATURES, OTHERS
AS SMALL AS GOATS – AND SOME
even as tiny as mice!

Traditionally, unicorns have been depicted as male.

DOES THIS MEAN THAT THERE ARE *no female unicorns?* OR THAT PERHAPS FEMALE UNICORNS ARE BETTER AT EVADING CAPTURE? THERE IS *no way to know for sure . . .*

44

Despite different attributes

ACROSS VARIOUS CULTURES, UNICORNS
ARE UNIVERSALLY BELIEVED TO BE

peaceful and kind.

The European unicorn

HAD A HORSE'S BODY, PEARLY WHITE COAT, AND LONG, WHITE, SPIRALLED HORN.

The Asian unicorn

HAD A SCALY, COLOURFUL COAT – OCCASIONALLY COVERED WITH MAGICAL SYMBOLS – A DEER'S BODY, AND A FLESH-COLOURED HORN.

The unicorn in Chinese mythology was called a qilin (PRONOUNCED *CHEE-LIN*). THE QILIN HAD A SCALY, DEER-LIKE BODY WITH A YELLOW BELLY AND SHINING, MULTI-COLOURED BACK, AND A DRAGON'S HEAD WITH ONE HORN. ACCORDING TO LEGEND, THE QILIN FIRST APPEARED IN THE GARDEN OF THE LEGENDARY YELLOW EMPEROR IN 2697 BCE. THIS BEAST WAS SO GENTLE, IT REFUSED TO EVEN WALK ON GRASS FOR FEAR OF HARMING IT.

THE APPEARANCE OF THIS MILD CREATURE foretold the birth or death of a wise ruler. IT IS SAID TO HAVE APPEARED TO THE PREGNANT MOTHER OF CONFUCIUS IN THE 6TH CENTURY BCE AND AGAIN BEFORE Confucius' death.

According to
Chinese legend,
THE ANCIENT PHILOSOPHER CONFUCIUS
WAS THE LAST PERSON EVER TO SEE
an Asian unicorn.

In Japan, the unicorn was called a kirin.

THIS WORD HAS NOW COME TO MEAN

'giraffe'

IN CONTEMPORARY JAPANESE, AFTER A 15TH-CENTURY AFRICAN EXPEDITION RETURNED AND OFFERED THE CHINESE EMPEROR

a live giraffe,

CALLING IT A UNICORN, AND THE WORDS BECAME FOREVER INTERLINKED!

THE KIRIN IS A REGAL AND
GENTLE ANIMAL, BUT WITH A

strong sense of justice,

DOLING OUT INSTANT PUNISHMENT
TO CRIMINALS WITH A SWIFT PIERCE OF

the horn through the heart.

ACCORDING TO EUROPEAN FOLKLORE,
A UNICORN COULD ONLY BE TAMED BY
a fair young maiden.
SHE NEED ONLY BE PURE, INNOCENT,
AND SIT ALONE IN A PICTURESQUE SCENE
(IDEALLY BESIDE A POMEGRANATE TREE).
UPON SEEING HER, THE WILD UNICORN
WOULD INSTANTLY CURL UP BESIDE HER AND
FALL ASLEEP WITH ITS HEAD IN HER LAP.

IN SOME TALES, THE UNICORN
sleeping peacefully
IN A MAIDEN'S LAP SYMBOLIZED
**the taming of
the unicorn.**
BUT IN OTHERS, A UNICORN COULD
ONLY BE CAUGHT AFTER A MAIDEN WAS
RATHER SAVAGELY THROWN BEFORE IT.
SADLY, THIS WAS OFTEN A TRAP SET IN
ORDER FOR HUNTERS TO CAPTURE
the wild beast.

'THE UNICORN, THROUGH ITS

intemperance

AND NOT KNOWING HOW TO CONTROL
ITSELF, FOR THE LOVE IT BEARS TO
*fair maidens, forgets its
ferocity and wildness;*
AND LAYING ASIDE ALL FEAR, IT WILL
GO UP TO A SEATED DAMSEL AND
GO TO SLEEP IN HER LAP, AND LET
THE HUNTERS TAKE IT.'

– LEONARDO DA VINCI

What sound do unicorns make?

THERE IS NO WAY TO KNOW FOR SURE. BUT SINCE THE BODY OF A UNICORN IS *closest to that of a horse,* IT'S LIKELY THE LARYNX (VOICE BOX) WOULD ALSO BE SIMILAR, PRODUCING THE SAME *NEIGH* SOUND. THEN AGAIN, A UNICORN ADDS MAGIC TO THE MIX, SO IT COULD ALSO SPEAK IN A HUMAN VOICE OR EVEN SOUND LIKE *the tinkling of bells!*

What do unicorns eat?

DEPICTIONS OF UNICORNS IN MEDIEVAL TAPESTRIES AND RENAISSANCE PAINTINGS SHOW THE MAGICAL BEASTS EATING GRASS FROM THE FOREST FLOOR, AS HORSES DO. ANOTHER THEORY IS THAT THESE OTHERWORLDLY CREATURES DO NOT REQUIRE FOOD AT ALL. INSTEAD, THEY ABSORB THE

sun's rays for their nourishment.

THEN TODAY'S POPULAR CULTURE WOULD
HAVE US BELIEVE THAT UNICORNS' DIET
CONSISTS ENTIRELY OF RAINBOW FOODS,
BRIMMING WITH SUGAR, SPRINKLES, AND
MINI MARSHMALLOWS. BUT UNTIL WE HEAR
IT DIRECTLY FROM THE UNICORN'S MOUTH,

*we'll have to keep
on imagining!*

LEGEND HAS IT THAT A UNICORN
STOPPED THE FEARSOME INVADER

Genghis Khan

FROM CONQUERING INDIA. AS THE WARRIOR
WAS PREPARING FOR THE INVASION,
a unicorn knelt
before him and gazed
into his eyes.

WITH NO OTHER EXPLANATION FOR WHAT
HE SAW THAN IT BEING A HEAVENLY SIGN,
Genghis Khan ordered
his army to retreat.

In spite of being fearless,

UNICORNS ARE SUPPOSEDLY SCARED
OF LABRADORS, BUT ESPECIALLY

*tame around
pheasants.*

The virtuous unicorn

IS SAID TO BE ABLE TO RECOGNIZE

liars instantly

AND WILL PIERCE SUCH INDIVIDUALS
THROUGH THE HEART WITH ITS HORN!

Saint Hildegard,

A 12TH-CENTURY GERMAN ABBESS,
WELL RESPECTED FOR HER TEACHINGS
ON MEDICINE AND SCIENCE,
recommended an
anti-leprosy ointment
MADE OF EGG YOLK AND *FOIE DE LICORNE*,
OR UNICORN LIVER.

The unicorn

EVEN APPEARS IN THE BIBLE AS A MAJESTIC ANIMAL CALLED A *RE'EM*, BASED ON TRANSLATIONS FROM SCHOLARS IN 300 BCE.

Modern translations now refer to this animal as a wild ox,

EXPLAINING THAT THE UNICORN WAS SIMPLY A TRANSLATION ERROR, BUT THE UNICORN HELD A SPECIAL SYMBOLIC MEANING FOR THE CHRISTIAN CHURCH EVEN SO.

The unicorn, with its peaceful but powerful nature, has symbolized Jesus.

JESUS IS SAID TO HAVE RAISED A UNICORN HORN AS A SYMBOL OF SALVATION FOR HUMANKIND. THE WORD 'UNICORN' OCCURS NINE TIMES IN THE KING JAMES BIBLE.

HOLY BIBLE

'SAVE ME FROM THE LION'S MOUTH: FOR THOU HAST HEARD ME FROM THE HORNS OF THE UNICORNS.'

– PSALMS 22:21, KING JAMES BIBLE

'GOD BROUGHT THEM OUT OF EGYPT;
HE HATH AS IT WERE THE STRENGTH
OF AN UNICORN.'

– NUMBERS 23:22, KING JAMES BIBLE

IN ANCIENT ASIA, UNICORNS WERE SEEN

*as bringers of
good luck.*

Unicorn horns

WERE BELIEVED TO CURE FEVERS,
NEUTRALIZE POISONS, PROLONG YOUTH, AND
act as an aphrodisiac
(love potion).

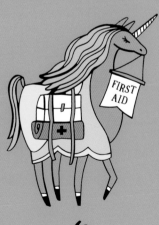

FIRST
AID

UNICORNS ARE BELIEVED TO HAVE **special powers,** INCLUDING PROTECTION, HEALTH, AND PURITY. THESE INCLUDE PROTECTION AGAINST STOMACH TROUBLE, EPILEPSY – AND EVEN THE PLAGUE. THOSE WHO DRANK FROM A UNICORN'S HORN WERE SAID TO BE PROTECTED FROM POISON, SINCE THE HORN WOULD PURIFY WHATEVER IT TOUCHED.

A unicorn could even purify a lake or stream by simply dipping its horn into the water.

IN APOTHECARIES ACROSS EUROPE,

unicorn horns

(OR 'ALICORNS') WERE AVAILABLE
FOR PURCHASE UNTIL THE 18TH CENTURY,
AS ONE OF THE MOST TRUSTED

health remedies.

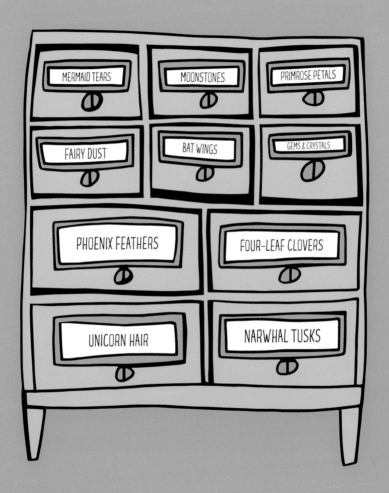

IN ADDITION TO ELIXIRS AND POWDERS,

items of unicorn clothing

WERE ALSO MEANT TO PROTECT
THE WEARER FROM MISFORTUNE AND
DISEASE. ADORNED IN UNICORN-LEATHER
SHOES AND A UNICORN BELT, THE
FASHIONABLE MEDIEVAL WEARER WOULD
EXPECT TO BE FREE OF DISEASE *AND*
THE PLAGUE — BUT LIKELY WITH

empty pockets, due to the high price tag.

Science

NICKNAMED THE
'Siberian unicorn',
ELASMOTHERIUM SIBIRICUM IS
THOUGHT TO HAVE LIVED ALONGSIDE
HUMANS 26,000 YEARS AGO. A HAIRY

*prehistoric rhinoceros
with a large horn,*

THIS ANIMAL'S SKELETON COULD HAVE
BEEN MISTAKEN FOR A UNICORN'S.

OTHER ANIMALS MISTAKEN FOR

unicorns

THROUGHOUT HISTORY INCLUDE THE
Indian rhinoceros,
narwhal, antelope,
and wild ox.

NICKNAMED 'SEA UNICORNS',

narwhals

HAVE LONG BEEN ASSOCIATED WITH
UNICORNS. WHILE THESE

small Arctic whales

SEEM OTHERWORLDLY, THEY ARE
DEFINITELY REAL.

FIG. 1

FIG. 2

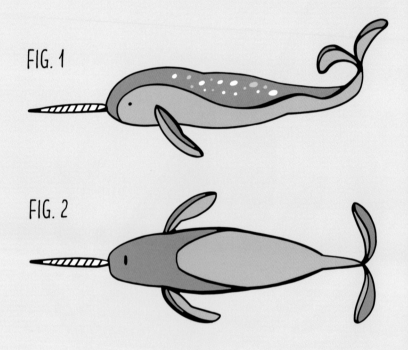

DID YOU KNOW?

Narwhals are small whales,

USUALLY FOUND IN THE ICY WATERS OF NORTHERN CANADA AND NORTHWESTERN GREENLAND. A MALE NARWHAL CAN WEIGH UP TO 1.8 TONNES (2 TONS) AND GROW UP TO 6 METRES (20 FEET) LONG. LIKE THEIR COUSINS, THE ORCA AND DOLPHIN, narwhals travel in large groups and eat mainly fish and shrimp.

THE STRAIGHT, TWISTED TUSK OF
THE NARWHAL IS ACTUALLY

a long tooth

THAT CAN MEASURE UP TO 3 METRES
(10 FEET) LONG IN MALES, GROWING
THROUGH THE UPPER LIP. (FEMALE
NARWHALS CAN ALSO GROW A VERY SMALL
TUSK.) THE NARWHAL TUSK ALWAYS GROWS

in a left-hand spiral.

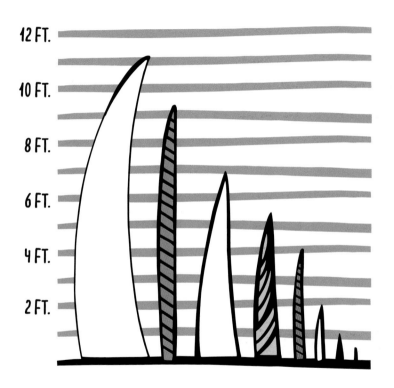

12 FT.

10 FT.

8 FT.

6 FT.

4 FT.

2 FT.

DID YOU KNOW?

THE JURY IS STILL OUT ON THE PURPOSE OF **the narwhal tooth.** ONE SCIENTIFIC THEORY IS THAT IT MAY BE ABLE TO DETECT WATER PRESSURE AND TEMPERATURE; ANOTHER IS THAT IT IS INVOLVED IN MATING *rituals or battles.*

Early descriptions

TOLD OF UNICORN HORNS IN A VARIETY OF COLOURS AND SIZES. BUT ONCE NARWHALS WERE DISCOVERED IN THE MIDDLE AGES AND SAILORS BEGAN TRADING THEM IN THE MARKETS OF EUROPE, SUDDENLY ALL 'UNICORN' HORNS STARTED LOOKING THE SAME: LONG, WHITE, AND SPIRALLED.

Let's see that narwhal tooth again . . .

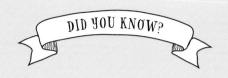

DID YOU KNOW?

UNICORNS CAN EVEN BE FOUND

in the sky.

THE CONSTELLATION *MONOCEROS* – GREEK FOR 'UNICORN' – HAS A MAGNITUDE OF 3.9. IT WAS DISCOVERED IN 1612 BY

the Dutch mapmaker Petrus Plancius.

THE EXISTENCE

# of unicorns

WAS ONLY DISPROVED IN 1825 BY THE
SCIENTIST BARON GEORGES CUVIER.

His proof?

THAT BIOLOGICALLY IT WAS IMPOSSIBLE
FOR AN ANIMAL WITH A SPLIT HOOF
(LIKE A HORSE) TO

*have a horn coming
from the top of
its head.*

A unicorn lair

WAS 'DISCOVERED' BY ARCHAEOLOGISTS
IN PYONGYANG, NORTH KOREA,
AS RECENTLY AS 2012.

The tip-off?

A CARVED ROCK AT THE ENTRANCE READING
'UNICORN LAIR' DATING FROM THE PERIOD
of Koryo Kingdom
(918—1392).

BAMBI, A DEER WITH

a single born

IN THE CENTRE OF ITS HEAD, WAS
BORN OUTSIDE FLORENCE, ITALY, IN
2008. THIS SINGLE HORN IS THE RESULT
OF A GENETIC MUTATION – RAISING THE
POSSIBILITY THAT ANIMALS WITH SIMILAR
MUTATIONS COULD HAVE BEEN SPOTTED
THROUGHOUT HISTORY, GIVING RISE TO

the legend of the unicorn.

UNICORNS ARE DEFINITELY REAL –

in finance.

A COMPANY (USUALLY TECH-BASED)
THAT IS LESS THAN TEN YEARS OLD
AND VALUED AT OVER $1 BILLION IS
CALLED A UNICORN BECAUSE IT WAS ONCE
SEEN AS THE STUFF OF MYTH.

Snapchat, Tinder, and Uber are modern-day unicorns!

THE WORD 'UNICORN' GOT AN EXTRA ENTRY
IN THE *COLLINS DICTIONARY* IN 2017.

That's right:

LISTED AFTER THE GLORIOUS MYTHICAL
HORNED CREATURE, YOU CAN NOW FIND
THE BUSINESS DEFINITION FOR UNICORN.

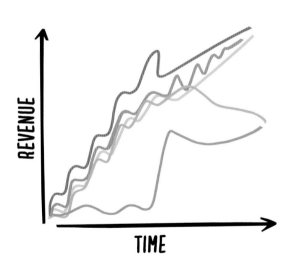

REVENUE

TIME

A unicorn skeleton

WAS 'FOUND' IN 1663 AT UNICORN CAVE IN THE HARZ MOUNTAINS IN GERMANY. LOCALS TRADED UNICORN BONES FROM THE CAVE, AND THE LOCAL MAYOR, RESPECTED NATURALIST AND INVENTOR OTTO VON GUERICKE, WROTE ABOUT THIS FIND, CONVINCED BY THE EVIDENCE.

The skeleton had only two legs, but a horse's head with a single horn.

IT WAS A JIGSAW OF A MAMMOTH, *narwhal, and woolly rhinoceros.* THE SKELETON CAN STILL BE SEEN TODAY AT THE ENTRANCE TO OSNABRÜCK ZOO, IN GERMANY.

'Artificial Production of the Fabulous Unicorn'?

THE ANSWER IS YES — ACCORDING TO A *SCIENTIFIC MONTHLY* ARTICLE PUBLISHED IN MAY 1936. THE BIOLOGIST DR. W. FRANKLIN DOVE EXPERIMENTED WITH CREATING AN ARTIFICIAL UNICORN BY USING SURGERY TO MOVE A YOUNG CALF'S HORNBUDS TO THE CENTRE OF ITS FOREHEAD.

This created a unicow!

THE COW BECAME THE LEADER OF HIS HERD AND DEVELOPED INTO A GENTLE BEAST, MUCH LIKE THE MYTHICAL UNICORN.

IN A SIMILARLY BIZARRE TALE,
live unicorns performed
AT SHOWS ACROSS THE USA IN THE 1980S
AS PART OF THE RINGLING BROS. AND
BARNUM & BAILEY CIRCUS.

'Lancelot the Unicorn'

MADE HIS DEBUT AT MADISON SQUARE
GARDEN IN NEW YORK CITY IN 1984.
THE CIRCUS TOLD THE PRESS THAT
LANCELOT AND HIS BROTHERS WERE

*'the only unicorns
in the world'*

AND THAT BECAUSE UNICORNS ARE
AGELESS, THEY COULD BE

'hundreds of years old'.

ON CLOSER INSPECTION, IT WAS SUGGESTED
THAT THEY WERE ACTUALLY GOATS THAT
HAD BEEN 'UNICORN-IFIED' AT A YOUNG
AGE, BUT THE CIRCUS DENIED THE CLAIM . . .

UNICORNS ARE NOT BORN BUT MADE . . .
THIS CLAIM WAS MADE BY OTTO ZELL,
THE NATURALIST WHO CREATED

Lancelot the goat-unicorn.

HE BELIEVED THAT ANCIENT AFRICAN
SHEPHERDS USED SIMILAR TECHNIQUES
AND DEVELOPED UNICORNS TO BE

herd leaders and protectors of the flock.

Art, Literature & Popular Culture

The collective noun for
a group of unicorns?
A blessing
OF UNICORNS.

'"Well, now that we have seen each other," said the unicorn, "if you'll believe in me, I'll believe in you."'

– *THROUGH THE LOOKING-GLASS, AND WHAT ALICE FOUND THERE,*
LEWIS CARROLL

POTIONS

UNICORN ANATOMY

SPELLS

The unicorn is noble,
He knows his gentle birth,
He knows that God has chosen him
Above all beasts of earth.

– GERMAN FOLK SONG

'Stars were golden unicorns neighing unheard through blue meadows spurning them with hooves sharp and scintillant as ice.'

– *SOLDIERS' PAY*, WILLIAM FAULKNER

'The unicorn lived in a lilac wood, and she lived all alone. She was very old, though she did not know it, and she was no longer the careless colour of sea foam, but rather the colour of snow falling on a moonlit night. But her eyes were still clear and unwearied, and she still moved like a shadow on the sea . . . [T]he mane that fell almost to the middle of her back was as soft as dandelion fluff and as fine as cirrus . . . and the long horn above her eyes shone and shivered with its own seashell light even in the deepest midnight.'

– *THE LAST UNICORN*, PETER S. BEAGLE

115

'Slowly the radiance took on form, until it had enfleshed itself into the body of a great white beast with flowing mane and tail. From its forehead sprang a silver horn which contained the residue of the light. It was a creature of utter and absolute perfection.'

– *A SWIFTLY TILTING PLANET,*
MADELEINE L'ENGLE

'A long time ago, when the earth was green,

There were more kinds of animals than you've ever seen.

They'd run around free while the earth was being born

And the loveliest of all was the unicorn.'

– *THE UNICORN*, SHEL SILVERSTEIN

WHILE UNICORNS HAVE
APPEARED THROUGHOUT HISTORY,
THEY HAVE NEVER BEEN

more popular

OR PERVASIVE THAN THEY ARE TODAY –
AND THAT'S THANKS IN PART TO SOCIAL
MEDIA. THE HASHTAG

#unicorn

IS AT 7 MILLION POSTS AND COUNTING.
ON PINTEREST, YOU CAN FIND TIPS
ON EVERYTHING FROM THROWING A
UNICORN PARTY TO MAKING YOUR OWN
*unicorn make-up, and
everything in between!*

According to Google, THE UNICORN HAS BEEN RISING IN POPULARITY SINCE 2015, SPIKING IN 2017 WITH THE LAUNCH OF STARBUCKS' UNICORN FRAPPUCCINO. THE UNICORN HAS BECOME A SYMBOL OF OUR TIMES, BOTH FOR ITS EMBODIMENT OF MAGIC AND BENEVOLENCE AND FOR ITS SHUNNING OF THE HARSH REALITY OF TODAY'S WORLD. THE UNICORN CAN BE SEEN EVERYWHERE – FROM UNICORN FRUIT LOOPS TO UNICORN SNOT BODY GLITTER, AND FROM FLUFFY SLIPPERS *to Gay Pride marches.*

'Unicornes may be betray'd with Trees.'

– DECIUS IN *JULIUS CAESAR*,
WILLIAM SHAKESPEARE (1599)

'Wert thou the Unicorne, pride and wrath would confound thee, and make thine owne self the conquest of thy fury.'

— TIMON IN *TIMON OF ATHENS*, WILLIAM SHAKESPEARE (1605)

UNICORNS MADE THEIR FIRST
APPEARANCE IN THE ARTWORK OF

Mesopotamia

(MODERN-DAY IRAQ) IN AROUND 500 BCE,
AS WELL AS IN THE ANCIENT MYTHS OF
India and China.

The Asian unicorn

MADE ITS FIRST APPEARANCE IN WRITTEN
STORIES FROM AROUND 2700 BCE AS A
*wild and powerful
creature.*

'A living drollery. Now I will believe that there are Unicornes, that in Arabia there is one tree, the Phoenix throne, one Phoenix at this hour reigning there.'

– SEBASTIAN IN *THE TEMPEST*, WILLIAM SHAKESPEARE (1610)

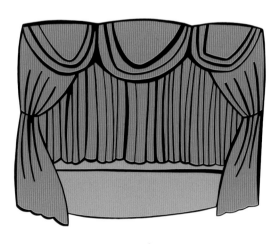

'It's not easy ter catch
a unicorn; they're
powerful magic creatures.
I never knew one ter
be hurt before.'

– RUBEUS HAGRID IN *HARRY POTTER AND
THE PHILOSOPHER'S STONE*, J.K. ROWLING

IN 2014, THE
'gender unicorn'
WAS BORN. IT IS A PURPLE UNICORN
CHARACTER THAT IS MEANT TO HELP
PEOPLE UNDERSTAND AND DESCRIBE THEIR
IDENTITY, INCLUDING GENDER IDENTITY
AND SEXUALITY. THE CONCEPT WAS
CREATED BY TSER (TRANS STUDENT
EDUCATIONAL RESOURCES) AND IS NOW
USED IN SCHOOLS AND UNIVERSITIES
around the world.

129

LEONARDO DA VINCI'S HOMETOWN OF VINCI, ITALY, HOSTS THE *FESTA DELL' UNICORNO*, OR

unicorn festival,

EVERY JULY. THE MEDIEVAL FANTASY FAIR INCLUDES EVERYTHING FROM HEAVY METAL BANDS TO COSPLAY COMPETITIONS, AND EVEN AN ELVEN WEDDING! ANYTHING GOES, SO LONG AS YOU DON'T BETRAY THE *'spirit of the unicorn'*.

'A wise man never plays leapfrog with a unicorn.'

TIBETAN PROVERB

THE LAST UNICORN IS A BEST-SELLING FANTASY NOVEL WRITTEN BY PETER S. BEAGLE ABOUT A BRAVE LITTLE UNICORN WHO BELIEVES SHE IS THE LAST OF HER KIND AND MUST EMBARK ON A QUEST TO DISCOVER WHAT HAPPENED TO THE OTHERS. READERS FELL IN LOVE WITH THE UNICORN AND HER RAGTAG CREW OF TALKING BUTTERFLIES, BUMBLING MAGICIANS, AND UNICORN DREAMERS. FIRST PUBLISHED IN 1968, IT HAS SOLD MILLIONS OF COPIES WORLDWIDE AND HAS BEEN TRANSLATED INTO 20 LANGUAGES.

FEATURING STARS SUCH AS CHRISTOPHER LEE, MIA FARROW, ANGELA LANSBURY, JEFF BRIDGES, AND ALAN ARKIN,

The Last Unicorn

HIT THE BIG SCREEN IN NOVEMBER 1982. IT BECAME AN INSTANT CULT CLASSIC, LOVED BY CHILDREN AND ADULTS ALIKE.

My Little Pony

FIRST LAUNCHED AS A TV SHOW AND CHILDREN'S TOY IN 1982. IN 2015, IT HAD A MASSIVE TV RELAUNCH AS *MY LITTLE PONY: FRIENDSHIP IS MAGIC*. THE HUGELY SUCCESSFUL *MY LITTLE PONY: THE MOVIE* HIT OUR SCREENS IN 2017.

The lead pony?

A Pegasus/unicorn cross named Princess Twilight Sparkle.

THE 2014 OSCAR-NOMINATED *LEGO MOVIE* FEATURED AN UNUSUAL UNICORN:

a pink cat-unicorn

CALLED PRINCESS UNIKITTY, THE RULER OF CLOUD CUCKOO LAND. UNIKITTY GOT HER OWN SPIN-OFF SHOW ON CARTOON NETWORK IN 2017.

The word 'unicorn' can be found around the globe:

AFRIKAANS: *BUFFEL*

ARABIC: *KARKADAN*

DUTCH: *EENHOORN*

ENGLISH: *UNICORN*

FRENCH: *LICORNE*

GAELIC: *AON-ADHARCACH*

GERMAN: *EINHORN*

GREEK: *MONOKEROS*

HEBREW: *HAD-KEREN*

POLISH: *JEDNOROŻEC*

SPANISH: *UNICORNIO*

SWAHILI: *NYATI*

Unicorn Crafts

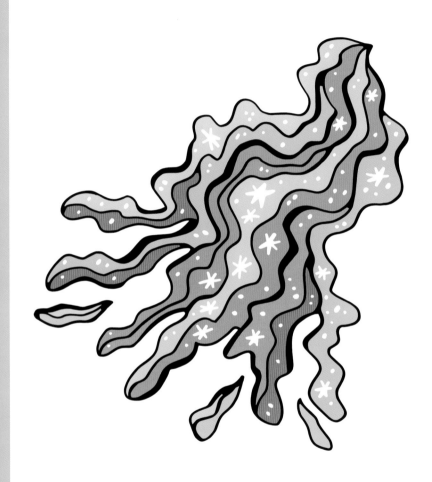

Unicorn snot slime

Looking for a simple craft project or a great gift idea? Look no further: unicorn snot slime is here! Just follow this simple recipe for DIY slime that is full of sparkle, colour and, most of all, fun. Add your own spin with glitter, sequins, tiny unicorn or star sprinkles – or any other bits of magic you like. Your imagination is the limit! This recipe is for single-colour slime; if you want a mix of colours, make one batch per colour and swirl them together at the end to create gorgeous rainbow slime.

Note: While this slime is borax-free and non-toxic, it is not edible.

Ingredients:

100 GRAMS (4 OUNCES) SQUEEZABLE NON-TOXIC WASHABLE CRAFT GLUE (GLITTER GLUE OR COLOURED GLUE OPTIONAL)

½ TBSP BICARBONATE OF SODA/ BAKING SODA

FOOD COLOURING (OPTIONAL)

1 TBSP CONTACT LENS SOLUTION (WITH BORIC ACID)

GLITTER, SEQUINS, OR OTHER DECORATIONS (OPTIONAL)

Equipment:

GLASS MIXING BOWL

METAL OR PLASTIC MIXING SPOON

AIRTIGHT PLASTIC BAG OR CONTAINER (FOR STORAGE)

Method:

1 Start by pouring the craft glue into a medium-sized bowl. This can either be measured out or squeezed directly from the bottle. An approximate measurement is fine.

2 Add the bicarbonate of soda/baking soda and use your spoon to mix well.

3 If you have used clear glue, this is your chance to add in food colouring to create whatever colour slime you choose. Mix thoroughly.

4 Now, squeeze in the contact lens solution and immediately start stirring with a spoon as the slime begins to take shape. Once the slime begins to look like, well, *slime*, start kneading it with your hands to ensure the same consistency throughout. If your slime is too sticky, add more solution and keep kneading until you get the desired texture.

5 If you are embellishing your slime with extra decorations, now is the time! Add the decorations in small amounts and mix thoroughly to make sure they are spread evenly throughout. If you have made separate batches of different-coloured slime, swirl them together now to create a rainbow. (Try to just swirl the separate colours. If you overmix, the colours will blend.)

6 Finally, store your slime in an airtight container to extend the fun!

Rainbow seed party favours

Whether you're throwing a birthday party or are in need of a quick and simple gift, a packet of rainbow seeds is certain to brighten anyone's day! Rainbow seeds are delightful in their joyful simplicity. All you need are your favourite rainbow sweets, small plastic bags, card or paper, markers, and any other decorations you like. A treat for humans, rainbow seeds are also instant unicorn food – and, with enough imagination, the seeds to grow a rainbow!

Materials:

SEVERAL SMALL CLEAR PLASTIC CRAFT BAGS (OR SMALL SANDWICH BAGS)

CARD OR CONSTRUCTION/ CRAFT PAPER

ONE BAG OF YOUR FAVOURITE MULTI-COLOURED SWEETS (SUCH AS SMARTIES, SKITTLES, OR SIMILAR)

Equipment:

MULTI-COLOURED MARKERS*

RAINBOW STAMP AND STAMP PAD (OPTIONAL)

GLITTER GLUE, SEQUINS, OR OTHER DECORATIONS (OPTIONAL)

STAPLER

*Note: Rather than drawing and writing out each tag, you may choose to design your rainbow seed tags on your computer and print them out instead. This can create a more uniform look and will make it quicker to produce a large number of gifts. This option will have a less homemade look than crafting each by hand.

145

Method:

1 First, prepare your bags. If you're using small craft bags, you're all set. But if you can only get your hands on small sandwich bags, cut off the tops to your chosen size.

2 Next, prepare your tags. For this, you'll need heavy-duty paper, such as card or construction/craft paper. You should be able to get several folded-over tags out of each sheet of paper, but the exact number will depend on the size of your bags. Measure your paper to ensure the tag is slightly wider than the top of the bag and cut out the strip of paper to fit, remembering that you'll want the strip twice the length, in order to fold over to cover both the back and front of the bag. Now carefully fold each strip in half. Continue until all of your tags are folded and ready to decorate.

3 Use your markers, stamps, and decorations to create each tag. Make sure each tag clearly states 'Rainbow seeds' and includes a picture of a rainbow, but other than that, make them as individual as you like! Why not stick on star sequins, use a rainbow stamp pad, or add stickers and sparkles?

4 When all of your bags and tags are ready, it's time for the sweets. Half-fill each bag with your rainbow sweets. Fold over a small lip at the top of the bag and use your stapler to seal it. Now slide your folded tag over the top of the sealed bag top, stopping when the bottom of your tag is in line with the top of the sweets. Use your stapler to neatly staple through the tag and bag in two or three places to attach.

5 *Voilà* – your lovely packets of rainbow joy are ready to share!

Fabulous unicorn headband/headphones

This crafting magic can be used to embellish anything! Why not try a simple headband or even headphones – or anything else you can think of . . . Adorn your lovely head with this fabulous creation to be instantly whisked from reality and into the wonders of unicorn land.

Materials:

WHITE, SILVER, OR GOLD FELT (OR ANY COLOUR OF YOUR CHOOSING), ROUGHLY 30CM² (5 SQ. IN.), MORE IF COVERING HEADPHONES

CRAFT STUFFING

PLASTIC HEADBAND, HEADPHONES, OR ANY OTHER HEAD ADORNMENT OF YOUR CHOOSING

FAKE FLOWERS, SEQUINS, RHINESTONES, RIBBONS, OR ANY OTHER DECORATIONS YOU CHOOSE

Equipment:

CRAFT GLUE OR A HOT-GLUE GUN

NEEDLE

SEWING THREAD (TO MATCH CHOSEN FELT COLOUR)

VELCRO SEW-ON TAPE, OR SIMILAR (OPTIONAL)

Method:

1 Let's start with the most important part: the alicorn, or unicorn horn. Cut out a long, narrow triangle of felt (roughly 12 centimetres/4 inches), snipping off the top, and two small circles (roughly 2.5 centimetres/1 inch in diameter) for sealing and attaching the horn. You can also cut additional circles for securing any of your larger additional embellishments (smaller ones should attach securely only using glue). Now glue along one long edge of the triangle and attach the other long edge, creating a long, tall, and cylindrical unicorn horn (or tall gnome's hat) shape. Leave it to dry for a few minutes. Gently turn the cone shape inside out so that the seam is on the inside. Fill the horn with stuffing, taking care not to create any lumps or bumps. Glue along the bottom edge of the circular base of your horn and press the felt circle onto the glue. Allow to dry for a few minutes. Now to create the trademark unicorn spiral. Thread your needle with the sewing thread. Pierce the tip of your horn with the needle and knot the end of the thread to secure it. In a spiral motion, wind the thread tightly along the length of the horn in the direction of the base. When you get to the bottom, pierce the felt and knot the thread, as you did at the top. You should now have an amazing and authentic spiralled unicorn horn!

2 If you're using a plastic headband, glue the circular base of the horn to the top centre of your headband. Glue the second felt circle to the underside of the headband, aligning it with the top felt circle. This will hide any glue and help to balance the horn.

If you're attaching your horn to headphones instead, I recommend not gluing this on directly and instead creating a removable 'sleeve'. Cut a rectangle out of your felt (roughly 10 centimetres/4 inches long and 5 centimetres/2 inches wide – or wide enough to cover the top of your headphones). Instead of gluing your unicorn horn's base and decorations directly onto the headband, glue them onto the centre of the rectangle. When you have completed your design, place the rectangle lengthways on the centre top of your headphones, with the horn positioned on the top of your head. On the bottom of the rectangle (on the underside of your headphones), tuck one long side of the felt underneath the other, ensuring that the felt is as tight as possible around the top of your headphones; this will show you where the closure is. Cut two pieces of Velcro tape the length of the rectangle. Apply glue along each long side, where the two sides overlap. Press each piece of Velcro on top of this glue. Allow to dry for several minutes. Now fold one long side of the rectangle over the other to secure the Velcro. Your headphones are now unicornified! When the time comes to remove your decoration, simply unpeel. You can reattach any time you want to re-adorn your headphones.

3 For any additional decorations, the design is up to you, but below are some tips for a few embellishments.

Ears: Use felt in a different colour to cut out small triangular ears. You can even cut out smaller pink triangles and glue those on top to create the inner ear, or cover the ear with glued-on glitter. Add glue along the bottom edge and attach to the top of the headband – or to your rectangular felt for the headphone design.

Flowers: Cut out flower petals or leaves from felt or paper and use glue to arrange around the base of your horn. Alternatively, try pre-made silk or felt flowers, or even dried ones. You can even find strings of flowers and leaves made of silk or felt that look lovely wrapped around the length of the headband.

Additional embellishments: Why not add ribbons, sequins, rhinestones, netting, or rainbow fake fur to your design?

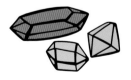

UNICORN SNOT
GLITTER GEL

DIY unicorn snot glitter gel

For a super simple and effective instant unicorn hit, look no further than DIY unicorn snot glitter gel!

This recipe couldn't be easier, and it's perfect for everything from a spot of party sparkle to an all-out unicorn glitter fest. Feel free to customize the colours and amount of glitter to suit your preferences. This recipe is for a light glitter dusting. If it's full-on glitter you're after, just add more loose glitter powder.

This recipe will make 1 tablespoon of glitter gel.

Ingredients:

LOOSE GLITTER POWDER* (CHOOSE COLOURS ACCORDING TO YOUR PREFERENCE; HOWEVER, A MIX OF COLOURS WORKS BEST) – ROUGHLY ⅛ TSP IN TOTAL FOR A 'FINER' GLITTER COVERAGE

APPROXIMATELY 1 TBSP CLEAR ALOE VERA GEL**

1–2 DROPS OF ESSENTIAL OIL, SUCH AS LAVENDER OR ROSE (OPTIONAL – THIS IS FINE TO USE IF YOU ARE APPLYING THE GLITTER TO YOUR SHOULDERS OR CHEEKS, BUT DO NOT APPLY TO THE EYELIDS)

*Loose glitter powder for the eyes and face, technically known as cosmetic-grade glitter (rather than craft glitter) can be found online, such as at Amazon, or at most cosmetic stores and counters, both as individual pots of colour and as sets. As with any make-up, please make sure to purchase through a reputable company and do a 'patch test' first. This involves testing a small amount on the inside of your elbow before applying to your face. This will allow you to know whether your skin is sensitive to the glitter.

**Aloe vera gel is a great moisturizer – but again, test out a small patch on your skin before using this unicorn snot glitter gel.

Equipment:

7 GRAMS (0.25 OUNCES) GLASS JAR
WITH LID*
COCKTAIL STICK/TOOTHPICK OR
COFFEE STIRRER

*Small round glass jars look great and are the easiest container to use for dabbing in your finger and applying the gel. However, you can experiment with squeezy travel shampoo tubes, if that's your preferred applicator, but you will need a small container with a wide opening for creating the glitter gel in the first place. Jars can be purchased at specialist cosmetic or craft stores, or found online.

Method:

1 First choose your glitter colours. Green, blue, and silver can be a gorgeous choice for a mermaid–unicorn crossover look, while a simple purple, white, and silver combination can look great as a subtle streak across the cheekbones. Prepare your colour palette and get ready to create.

2 Add 1 tablespoon of aloe vera gel to your glass jar or other chosen container. Add a tiny pour or pinch of glitter in each of your chosen colours. Add one colour at a time, starting with the darker colours first (you can always lighten it back up using white or silver at the end). The first time you do this, measure your glitter so that you don't accidentally pour in too much. The more you practise, the better you will become at knowing how much you need. After adding each colour, use your stirrer to mix the glitter in thoroughly. This will produce a 'fine' glitter dusting on your skin. Test this on a patch of skin to see if you are happy with the effect. If you prefer a denser glitter covering, add more glitter at this stage. If you are including an essential oil, add 1 drop at a time now and stir thoroughly.

3 That really is it. Glitter up, glam out, and sparkle to your heart's content!

Unicorn DIY bath bombs

Fancy soaking up some magical unicorn goodness, while relaxing in a warm and soothing bubble bath? Of course you do! And what makes it even better is that you can make these luxurious bath bombs at home, either to keep for yourself or to give as cherished homemade gifts. Customize your bath bombs to include your favourite scents, colours, and added embellishments. These bath bombs are gorgeous, indulgent, and – best of all – simple to make!

This recipe will produce roughly 2–3 bath bombs, depending on the size of your chosen mould.

Ingredients:

220 GRAMS (1 CUP) BICARBONATE OF SODA/BAKING SODA

120 GRAMS (½ CUP) CITRIC ACID*

120 GRAMS (½ CUP) EPSOM SALTS**

120 GRAMS (½ CUP) CORNFLOUR/ CORN STARCH

2½ TBSP ALMOND OIL

¾ TBSP WATER

2 TSP ESSENTIAL OIL OF YOUR CHOOSING, SUCH AS LAVENDER, PEPPERMINT, PATCHOULI, VANILLA

FOOD COLOURING

LUSTRE DUST***, SPRINKLES, FLOWER PETALS (OPTIONAL – JUST ENSURE THEY ARE FOOD GRADE OR ALL NATURAL)

*Citric acid is a naturally occurring substance found in citrus fruit, as well as many other fruits and vegetables. It is also a common food additive. Citric acid can be found in large supermarkets/grocery stores or specialist stores, and is usually stocked alongside other preservatives, such as pectin, for making jams and preserves.

**Epsom salts are available in many supermarkets/grocery stores and pharmacies. It can be found either in the first-aid section or next to other bath products. Epsom salts available through these outlets will meet regulatory standards for safe human use. While both ingredients are heavily tested and regulated and non-toxic for human ingestion, it is best to avoid consuming these ingredients.

***Lustre dust can be sourced online or from the baking section of a supermarket/grocery or specialist store.

Equipment:

MEDIUM OR LARGE SIEVE

AT LEAST 2 MIXING BOWLS (YOU NEED
ONE BOWL FOR EACH COLOUR YOU'D LIKE
FEATURED IN YOUR BATH BOMB)

WHISK

RUBBER GLOVES

BATH BOMB MOULD*

BAKING PARCHMENT OR KITCHEN ROLL/
PAPER TOWEL

*Bath bomb moulds are available at craft stores and can be easily ordered online, at sites such as Amazon. A spherical mould will give you the traditional bath bomb shape, but it will only produce one bomb at a time. For a quick and easy alternative that will produce several bath bombs at a time, why not try a stainless-steel muffin tin or even plastic Easter eggs?

Method:

1 Begin by placing a sieve over a mixing bowl. Add each dry ingredient at a time – the bicarbonate of soda/baking soda, citric acid, Epsom salts, and cornflour/corn starch – using the sieve to sift. This will ensure the ingredients are better blended. Use a whisk to thoroughly stir through until the ingredients are evenly combined.

2 Use a second mixing bowl to combine your wet ingredients: almond oil, water, and any scented essential oil or oils of your choosing. With practice, you can discover some great aroma combinations.

3 Now for the science! This part requires careful concentration to produce a delicate and refined bath bomb. If you're too impatient, the ingredients will react, and you'll end up with a lumpy, bumpy bomb . . . Very slowly add the wet mixture to the dry. In order to keep the process slow and steady, I recommend pouring or spooning in a small amount of the wet mixture at a time, stirring quickly and thoroughly. Repeat until all of the wet and dry mixtures have been combined and the mixture resembles wet sand.

4 Separate the mixture into your assortment of clean mixing bowls. Start with one bowl and add a drop of food colouring at a time. Use a gloved hand to thoroughly knead the colour through the mixture, repeating this process until the mixture is your chosen colour. Wash your glove before starting on the next colour in a separate bowl. You will end up with bowls of assorted colours of 'wet sand'.

5 The next step is creating the shape. The instructions vary slightly depending on the type of mould being used. If using a spherical bath bomb mould, begin with one colour packed into the bottom of the mould as a layer. Alternate your colours, packing the mixture firmly into the top and bottom of your mould. Make sure that you slightly overfill the two halves, as this will ensure that there is no gap and will provide a tighter fit. When you're done, press the two halves together firmly and leave to harden. If you're using a muffin tin, follow the same process, layering firmly into the bottom of each cup. Pack the mixture in solidly, but do not use any additional implements to pack it in, as this will make the bomb difficult to remove.

6 Cover your work surface with a layer of baking parchment or kitchen roll/paper towel. Now remove your bombs from their moulds. If using a spherical mould, gently tap the mould on a solid surface to loosen it before carefully opening the top and bottom of the mould. Gently remove the bomb from the mould and place it on the covered work surface. If using a muffin tin, very gently and evenly tap the bottom of the tin on a solid surface. Turn the tin upside down and very carefully tap the bottom of each cup to remove the bomb from its holder and onto the covered surface. If you would like added sparkle, add lustre dust to the top or surface of your bomb. Allow the bombs to dry and harden for 48 hours.

7 Your gorgeous DIY unicorn bath bombs are now ready to use or to share! If not using right away, ensure the bombs are kept dry by sealing in a plastic bag or container.

Unicorn Rainbow Food Recipes

Unicorn hot chocolate

Prep time: 10–15 minutes   Serves 2

A super-quick unicorn food fix? Why, unicorn hot chocolate, of course! This rich, delicious, and – most importantly – pastel-hued rainbow fix is certain to bring sunshine to even the coldest of winter days. It is quite simply sprinkle-topped magic in a mug. Feel free to 'magic up' your drink to your heart's content. Think: sprinkles, crushed candy cane, popping candy, mini marshmallows, edible gold flakes – even the shaped marshmallows you get in some sugary breakfast cereals! – then sip away and drift off into a rainbow fug of contentment. You're welcome.

Note: This recipe calls for solid white or milk chocolate. For an even quicker recipe, consider using pre-made hot chocolate mix for the base.

Ingredients:

50 GRAMS (2 OUNCES) WHITE OR MILK CHOCOLATE BAR, CHOPPED INTO SMALL PIECES

200 MILLILITRES (7 FLUID OUNCES) WHOLE/FULL-FAT MILK

FOOD COLOURING OF YOUR CHOICE

FOOD COLOURING GEL (OPTIONAL)

YOUR CHOICE OF MINI MARSHMALLOWS, COLOURED SWEETS, AND/OR SPRINKLES

To serve:

100 MILLILITRES (3½ FLUID OUNCES) DOUBLE CREAM/HEAVY CREAM (IF MAKING IT FROM SCRATCH) OR WHIPPED CREAM IN A SPRAY CAN

Equipment:

DISPOSABLE PIPING BAG (IF USING)

SAUCEPAN

SPOON

PASTEL OR UNICORN-THEMED MUGS

163

Method:

1 First, prepare your embellishments. This ensures the drinker does not end up sipping beautifully adorned *cold* chocolate. If you're using ready whipped cream, have this to hand. If you're making your own whipped cream, prepare this first by whipping double/heavy cream with a whisk and lots of arm muscle until it forms sturdy peaks on the surface. You can then decorate the inside of a disposable piping bag with food colouring, to create rainbow-striped cream. Or you can get creative with cake airbrush kits to spray on colour or swirl or dot on colour directly using the food colouring pipette onto the whipped cream. Plan and do all of this in advance.

2 Now to make the hot chocolate. Chop up the chocolate bar into small pieces, or crumble it with your hand.

3 Next, pour the milk into a small saucepan and simmer until it starts to lightly bubble, stirring with a heatproof spoon throughout. Keep the heat low and add the chocolate, continuing to stir until the chocolate has completely melted. The liquid should be thick and even. Take the pan off the heat. If using white chocolate, add food colouring of your choice to create pastel-coloured deliciousness. Carefully pour the mixture into two mugs.

4 To decorate your creation, top with the cream of your choosing. If using DIY whipped cream, you can add it to the pre-prepared piping bag with a wide tip; otherwise, squeeze your ready-made whipped cream directly on top of the surface of the drink. Pile on the mini marshmallows, sprinkles, silver edible balls, popping candy, or anything else your unicorn heart desires. Enjoy!

165

Breakfast magic rainbow pancakes

Prep time: 10 minutes   Serves 4
Makes 20 × 7.5-centimetre- (3-inch)-round pancakes

In our household, these delicious pancakes – in their traditional-brown form, served with lashings of maple syrup – are a quick and easy weekend treat. So beloved were they in my family from my youngest days, my toddler self could often be heard requesting more 'cookies' (tiny pancakes)! Life was always good with a 'cookie' in each hand. I'd like to share with you our family recipe – with added unicorn magic. I present to you Breakfast Magic Rainbow Pancakes! This tasty treat is sure to add a touch of magic to any morning, and is particularly helpful on a grey and rainy Sunday. For double the rainbow, why not accompany with rich and delicious unicorn hot chocolate?

A special thank you goes to my mom and my aunt Marie for introducing me to this recipe all those years ago.

Ingredients:

6 LARGE EGGS

350 GRAMS (1 ½ CUPS) COTTAGE CHEESE

½ TSP TABLE SALT

¼ TSP BAKING POWDER

65 GRAMS (½ CUP) PLAIN/
ALL-PURPOSE FLOUR

COOKING SPRAY OR BUTTER, TO GREASE

FOOD COLOURING

BUTTER, TO SERVE (OPTIONAL)

MAPLE SYRUP, TO SERVE (OPTIONAL)

A RAINBOW ARRAY OF FRUIT OR SWEET
DECORATIONS, TO SERVE (OPTIONAL)

Equipment:

GRIDDLE PAN OR LARGE FLAT
FRYING PAN

BLENDER OR FOOD MIXER
(OR LARGE MIXING BOWL
AND WHISK)

SEVERAL SMALL MIXING BOWLS
FOR EACH CHOSEN COLOUR

LADLE

SPATULA

LARGE PLATTER OR
INDIVIDUAL PLATES,
TO SERVE

Method:

1 If you're adding fruit or sweet decorations, prepare these in advance. Chop up a rainbow of raspberries, strawberries, bananas, kiwis, and blueberries to embellish your rainbow pancakes with a tasty – and healthy – topping. Or add rainbow sprinkles or other sweet decorations for a more sugary treat!

2 Add the eggs, cottage cheese, salt, baking powder, and flour to the mixer and blend at high speed for 20 seconds. Alternatively, add all of these ingredients to a large bowl and whisk well, until the batter is an even consistency.

3 Distributing evenly, pour the batter into each of the individual bowls. Add one drop of each chosen food colour to each bowl, stirring thoroughly with a whisk or spoon. Build up the colour gradually by adding another drop at a time, until you get the shade you want. (Note: a little food colouring goes a long way!) Rinse your whisk or spoon between each bowl so as not to mix colours. Carry out the same step for each colour of batter. You will now have a rainbow of different colours of pancake batter.

4 Evenly grease the pan and place over a medium heat on the hob, until the butter or spray begins to crackle very slightly.

5 Use a ladle to spoon the batter onto the hot pan, creating pancakes of your chosen size. (The batter will spread out slightly on the hot surface, but a general rule of thumb is that a soup-spoon-size amount will create a 'silver dollar'-size pancake roughly 6 centimetres/2 inches in diameter; a half-ladle-full will create a large pancake. Allow space between each pancake.) When small air bubbles begin to form around the edge of the pancakes, use a spatula to flip them over, browning the other side. Take care not to burn the second side – the cooking time is less on the second side than the first, but the timing depends on your chosen pancake size. For better control of timings, cook one colour of pancake at a time in a small batch, ladling out the next batch when the first is done. The first batch can work as a tester for timings.

6 Pile up your rainbow pancakes on a platter or individual plates. Serve with butter, syrup, or top with your chosen fruit or sweet decorations. In the unlikely event that you have any leftover pancakes, store in an airtight bag or container in the fridge for up to four days.

Unicorn Bark

A magical spin on the wintry peppermint treat, unicorn bark makes a great gift – that is, if it lasts long enough to share! It's both delicious and almost too gorgeous to eat, except that you won't be able to resist . . . This treat can be personalized to anyone's taste, too. The world is your rainbow when it comes to experimenting with colours, flavours, toppings, and sweets – from traditional candy-cane peppermint to rose and violet lusciousness.

Note: The melted chocolate will be hot, so take care while handling it.

Ingredients:

500 GRAMS (18 OUNCES) HIGH-QUALITY WHITE CHOCOLATE BAR (BROKEN INTO SQUARES) OR EQUIVALENT MEASURE OF WHITE CHOCOLATE CHIPS

MIX OF FOOD COLOURING OF YOUR CHOICE

ADDITIONAL FLAVOURING, SUCH AS LAVENDER, ROSEWATER, OR PEPPERMINT (OPTIONAL)

EMBELLISHMENTS OF YOUR CHOICE (SPRINKLES, CRYSTALLIZED VIOLET, CRUSHED CANDY CANE, JELLY DROPS, MINI MARSHMALLOWS – ANY SWEET ADORNMENTS THAT WON'T MELT TOO QUICKLY, UNLESS THAT'S YOUR DESIRED EFFECT)

Equipment:

LARGE BAKING TRAY

BAKING PARCHMENT (OPTIONAL)

GLASS OR METAL BOWLS FOR EACH CHOSEN CHOCOLATE COLOUR

MICROWAVE AND OVEN GLOVE

WHISK OR BAKING SPOON

COCKTAIL STICKS/TOOTHPICKS

AIRTIGHT CONTAINER AND/OR GIFT BOXES

Method:

1 Prepare your embellishments and set them aside in separate bowls, so that they are ready and waiting when the time comes to decorate (and before the chocolate begins to set too much!). Set up as many individual empty bowls as you need for each chosen colour of chocolate, so that everything is ready in advance. Prepare your baking tray in advance by lining it with parchment paper (if using) and setting aside.

2 Measure out your chocolate and add to a microwaveable, heat-proof bowl. Heat the chocolate in the microwave in short intervals (20 to 30 seconds) until melted. After each burst, use an oven glove to remove from the microwave and stir the chocolate. Once the chocolate has thoroughly melted, again use an oven glove to remove the bowl from the microwave and stir thoroughly until the chocolate is melted and smooth all over. If you are choosing to add an additional flavouring, such as peppermint or rose (and you would like all of the bark flavoured the same throughout), add three drops of your chosen flavouring now. Stir thoroughly. (If you prefer a stronger flavour, add another drop – however, the strength of the flavour will depend on your chosen flavouring and particular brand.) If you would prefer each colour to be a different flavour, wait until the melted chocolate has been divided into separate bowls, then add the flavouring after the food colouring (adding only one drop per bowl), stirring thoroughly.

3 Pour the melted chocolate evenly between your empty bowls. Starting with one drop at a time, add a different colour of food colouring to each bowl and mix well. By starting with a small amount of colouring and adding it gradually, you can better control the colour of your chocolate. A small amount will create a pastel shade; more will make a bolder colour. Stir thoroughly to ensure the colour is even.

4 Now spoon, or carefully pour, drips or blobs of each colour of chocolate onto the baking tray. They will start to run into each other. Gently tip the baking tray from one side to the other to ensure the chocolate covers the entire base of the tray.

5 Now for your own individual design: you can either leave your colours as individual 'spots' if you prefer, or you can use a cocktail stick to delicately swirl them together and create a marbled effect.

6 And finally: decorations! Use the embellishments you chose to decorate your tray of rainbow chocolate. Add mini marshmallows, sprinkles, sweets, crystallized flower petals – anything! (Remember that if you chose chocolate, such as chocolate chips or chocolate buttons, these will melt slightly onto the melted chocolate base.) It's up to you if you lightly sprinkle each topping across the entire chocolate base or if you prefer to have different patches with different toppings.

7 Leave the tray of chocolate overnight in a cool place, such as the fridge, to set. Once it is solid, use your hands to break it into uneven pieces – or (very delicately) pound with a meat tenderizer wrapped in a clean tea towel. The bark can be stored in an airtight container in the fridge for up to a week – or given out as a gift in pretty plastic gift bags or boxes. That is, if you find yourself able to share!

Rainy day unicorn milkshake

Prep time: 10 minutes   Serves 2

Perhaps you've just passed a particularly tough exam, or spent the day clearing out under your bed . . . Whether good or bad, there's always a reason to be found for a reward or a cheer-up treat. And what could be better than rainbow goodness wrapped around ice cream, with lashings of sprinkles and whipped cream, to be sipped through a straw? Very little, if you ask me. Go on, there's time to think of a reason while you're prepping this treat . . .

Note: This recipe includes two coloured layers. Why not experiment and come up with your own colours and flavours for additional layers?

175

Ingredients:

2 LARGE SCOOPS (2 CUPS) VANILLA ICE CREAM

90 MILLILITRES (3 FLUID OUNCES) WHOLE MILK

60 MILLILITRES (2 FLUID OUNCES) RED SYRUP (SUCH AS STRAWBERRY OR RASPBERRY FLAVOURED SYRUP)*

60 MILLILITRES (2 FLUID OUNCES) BLUE SYRUP (SUCH AS BLUEBERRY OR BLUE RASPBERRY)*

*IF YOU PREFER THE TASTE OF A VANILLA MILKSHAKE, USE 2–3 DROPS OF FOOD COLOURING INSTEAD

To serve:

WHIPPED CREAM

DECORATIONS (SPRINKLES, MINI MARSHMALLOWS, CHERRIES AND BLUEBERRIES, POPPING CANDY)

Equipment:

ICE-CREAM SCOOP OR SPOON

BLENDER

METAL SPOON

TALL CLEAR GLASS

STRAW OR LONG SPOON

Method:

1 Add half of the ice cream and half of the milk, as well as the red syrup or 2–3 drops of red food colouring, to the blender. Mix well until smooth. Pour this mixture carefully into a tall glass, avoiding the sides.

2 Clean the blender before the next step.

3 In the blender, mix the remaining ice cream and milk with the blue syrup or 2–3 drops of blue food colouring. Again, mix well until smooth.

4 'Float' the blue mixture on top of the red layer. Do this by pouring the mixture over the back of the metal spoon and against the side of the tall glass. Ensure you allow room in the glass for your toppings.

5 Finish by topping the milkshake with whipped cream, sprinkles, cherries and blueberries, and any other decorations that you choose. Serve with a straw or long spoon and bask in your well-earned reward. Now back to that reason . . . Have you thought of one yet?

Extraordinary rainbow party cake

Prep time (to include baking): 1.5–2 hours
(depending on previous cake-icing experience)

Serves 10–12

Makes a cake 20 centimetres (8 inches)
across with six layers

This cake is, quite simply, stunning. It's also a party on a plate! While the overall time it takes may seem like a drag, trust me – it's so worth it. The cake will look like a masterpiece, but each individual step really is simple and easy to follow. Make this cake for a special birthday, and it will be the heart of the party. Your friends will be clamouring for more, begging for the recipe. I love the way the simple, pure white icing masks the hidden wonder underneath. But if you would prefer your cake's outer self to reflect the party going on inside, feel free to add food colouring to the icing, too.

A very special thank you goes to the lovely Aunty Becs for sharing her fantabulous rainbow recipe!

Cake

Note: The ingredients and method here are for two cakes at a time. Multiply the ingredients by three for the total of what you'll need for the six-layer cake.

For each set of two cakes:

125 GRAMS (4.5 OUNCES) SOFT MARGARINE (PLUS A LITTLE EXTRA FOR GREASING THE CAKE TINS)

225 GRAMS (1¾ CUPS) PLAIN/ALL-PURPOSE FLOUR

150 GRAMS (¾ CUP) GOLDEN CASTER/SUPERFINE SUGAR

3 MEDIUM EGGS

1 TSP BAKING POWDER

1 TSP VANILLA EXTRACT

EDIBLE FOOD COLOURING OR GEL COLOURING (GEL CAN CREATE BRIGHTER COLOURS) IN RED, ORANGE, YELLOW, GREEN, BLUE, AND PURPLE (THESE COLOURS ARE FOR ALL SIX CAKES.)

Equipment:

2 × 20-CENTIMETRE (8-INCH) 'SANDWICH' CAKE TINS

BAKING PARCHMENT

LARGE MIXING BOWL AND ELECTRIC HAND WHISK, OR ELECTRIC MIXER

ANOTHER LARGE MIXING BOWL

KITCHEN SCALES

PLASTIC OR RUBBER BAKING SPATULA OR ICING SPREADER

WOODEN SKEWER OR COCKTAIL STICKS/TOOTHPICKS

2 WIRE COOLING RACKS

Method:

1 Pre-heat the oven to 180°C/160°C fan-assisted/350°F. Set up your cooling racks in advance.

2 To save time, make two cakes (or layers) at a time. First, line the bases of your two cake tins with baking parchment and grease the sides with margarine.

3 Add all the cake ingredients (except for the food colouring) to your mixing bowl or electric mixer and beat until smooth.

4 Weigh your cake batter and pour half into a separate bowl. Now add one colour of food colouring to each bowl and mix thoroughly. Make sure you wash the whisk after each colour before going on to mix the next. Start with one drop of food colouring at a time and build up the colour gradually, mixing after each addition. Continue until you have the desired colour. (This will be quite true to the colour of the final baked cake layer.) Pour the cake batter into each of your two cake tins and use a baking spatula or icing spreader to smooth the top of the mixture.

5 Bake both cake layers in the oven for approximately 12 minutes (or until a wooden skewer poked into the centre of the cake comes out clean). Carefully turn the cakes out onto the wire racks to cool.

6 Wash the cake tins, bowls, and mixing equipment thoroughly and ensure that they are cool before proceeding. You are now all set to repeat steps 2 to 5 for the rest of the colour layers. Once finished, leave all six layers to cool thoroughly. Now onto the icing . . .

Icing

Ingredients:

125 GRAMS (1 STICK, OR 4.5 OUNCES)
SOFTENED BUTTER

350 GRAMS (2¾ CUPS) SIFTED ICING
SUGAR/POWDERED SUGAR

A FEW DROPS OF VANILLA OR LEMON
FLAVOURING (WHICHEVER YOU PREFER)

3–4 TBSP WARM WATER

Equipment:

MEDIUM MIXING BOWL

HAND WHISK, OR ELECTRIC MIXER

RUBBER SPATULA OR ICING SPREADER

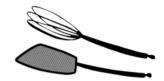

Method:

1 Add the butter to the bowl or electric mixer, and beat until it is a soft, creamy texture. Gradually add the sugar, mixing thoroughly. Next add enough water to create the desired icing consistency. If it is too dry, add more water; if too wet, add more icing sugar.

2 When all six cake layers have cooled thoroughly, you may begin icing. Start with the purple cake layer on the bottom, and spread a layer of icing evenly across the top. Next place the blue cake layer on top and ice evenly across the top. Next add the green cake layer, followed by the yellow, orange, and red, repeating the icing process with each layer, until all six cake layers have been sandwiched together into one cake. This is your rainbow cake!

3 Finally, evenly cover the entire cake with the remaining icing. A useful tip is to first use a thin, all-over layer of icing to catch any crumbs and to even out any nooks and crannies in the surface. Follow with a second layer of icing that will be your smooth outer layer.

4 *Voilà*! Your gorgeous rainbow cake is done and ready to be served – to the *oohs* and *ahs* of your delighted cake-eaters!

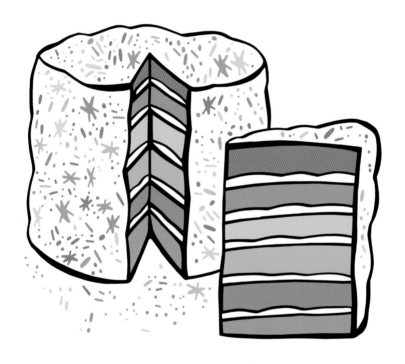

Unicorn
Spells &
Charms

Unicorn magic & you

The most powerful magic in the universe is the power of our minds. This might sound too simple, but it's true! Our minds are more powerful than we could ever imagine, but sometimes, we forget this is the case. For example, imagine that you've planned something – say, a visit to a friend. But something goes wrong, and the visit can't happen. Your immediate reaction is likely to be upset or anger. However, after that first reaction, you have a choice. You can choose to continue being upset (which isn't really helpful), or you can choose to look at things another way, and try to find either a solution or an alternative. This is down to the power of your mind – and this is what true magic is all about.

Magical spells of all kinds rely on a focused mind. Put simply, human beings use symbols in any type of magic to help focus the mind and individual intentions. If you've ever been inside a religious building of any kind, you will have seen examples of items that we as humans have used for thousands of years for exactly this purpose. Think of statues, pictures, candles, fragrances, repeated words, and the singing of songs. (Songs in particular are often so well known that we forget about the meaning of the words.) A prayer, or mantra, is a very powerful kind of magic, used in different religions all over the world. Colours, too, can affect our moods, and we often don't even realize it.

So, you might be thinking, what has this got to do with unicorns, and unicorn magic? The answer is *EVERYTHING*! The following spells and charms all use the magical unicorn as their focus for good intentions. So, knowing exactly what the unicorn stands for will help you think more clearly and focus your energy.

Before you proceed, take a piece of paper and write down everything a unicorn means to you, including any words that you associate with the mystical beasts.

Think about images of unicorns that you have seen, and pick out anything that holds meaning for you.

Your list might include words such as virtue, honesty, purity, beauty, gentleness, innocence, childhood, kindness – really, anything at all. The unicorn often appears with rainbows, or standing calmly in a forest, so include ideas and images like these that are meaningful to you, as well as any colours – or even any other descriptions of the senses that an image of a unicorn raises for you. The colour white is often associated with unicorns, since white is also the colour for purity.

In the same way that churches and other places of religious worship have an altar, you can design a unicorn altar for yourself, which will be the focus of your magical practice.

Find a small space that you can use for your altar. Make sure it is thoroughly clean and sparkling both before your ritual and after it. Put appropriate objects on the altar – you could use a unicorn picture that you've drawn or cut out, or a statue of the animal. Consider a small pot of fresh wild flowers, or leaves from the sort of place a unicorn would like to live. Perhaps a scented candle in a candle stick, or a tealight in a jar. You might have other little charms or trinkets that are meaningful to you, so include these.

Now you're ready to do some magic.

PHOTOS

PEN + PAPER

CANDLES

FLOWERS

WATER

TRINKETS

COINS

SALT

188

Unicorn Spell for Removing Unhappiness

Unicorn spell for removing unhappiness

Light the candle on your altar (a white one is good for this purpose) and arrange everything in a way that works for you. You will need to add a small dish of salt. This is used to absorb negative energies.

Take a piece of paper and a pen. Thinking hard, and using one word per item, ask the unicorn to help you think of all the things that make you unhappy, then write them down in a list. Don't try to analyze anything, just write as it comes to you. Write until you've run out of ideas. The unicorn will tell you when it's time to stop.

Then, sit for a few minutes, watching the peaceful flickering of the candle. When you're ready, take the list, and read each item out loud. Now apply your mind to each item; can you do anything about it? Can you change your mind about how something makes you feel? Maybe the thing you've written down doesn't seem so bad on paper? When you're done, imagine that each one of the words is inside a bright-pink balloon. Now take a deep breath and blow all the balloons away until they're completely out of sight.

Throw away the salt and then blow out the candle. Tear up the piece of paper, and take it outside to burn.

Unicorn Spell for Happiness

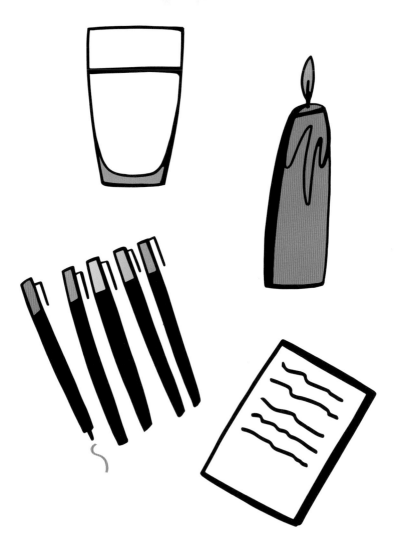

Unicorn spell for happiness

Return to your altar. Light a candle (a pink one is good for this purpose) and arrange everything how you like it. You will need to add a small glass of water. The water is used to absorb positive energies.

Take a piece of paper and pens of several different rainbow colours. Without thinking too hard, ask the unicorn to help you think of all the things that make you happy, and write them down, using the colour that feels most appropriate for each item. Write down as many things as you can think of. There might be some things on the list that you love to do, but that you might not have done for a long time; include them anyway. There might be people who you love to spend time with, but you haven't seen for a while; list them. There might be hobbies or crafts that you enjoy, but which you don't make time for; add them.

Spend some time looking over your list. Are there items that surprised you? Take as much time as you need to reflect on your list. Now take the list and pin it up where you can see it every day. Plan to spend more time doing the happy things that you've written down.

Drink the water and blow out the candle.

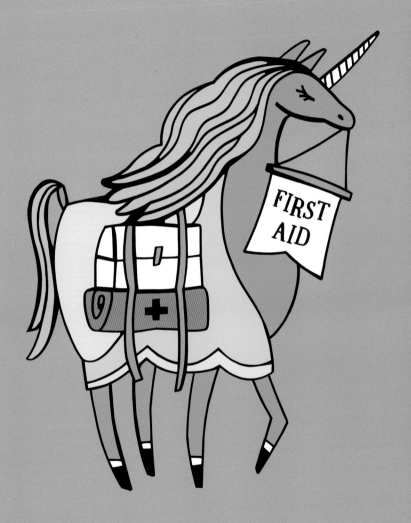

Unicorn Spell for Health

Unicorn spell for health

Return again to your altar. Light a candle (green is a good colour for this purpose) and arrange everything in a way that feels right to you. You will need to add an apple, a piece of paper, and some pens.

Gaze into the flickering light of the candle and ask your body to tell you what is good for it, and the things that it needs. Concentrate on the flame, and let your mind calm down, allowing your instincts and intuition – with the help of the unicorn – to take over. At first it might seem as though nothing is happening, but persevere, and soon words will begin to come to you. However strange they might seem, write them down. It might be that certain foods come into your head, or specific types of exercise. Perhaps you think of vitamins. Or maybe you'll be told to eat foods of a certain colour. Maybe your instinct suggests something really simple, such as spending more time outside. Listen to what your instinct and intuition are telling you.

Write down the things that seem the most important, and make it your resolution to do some of those things.

Eat the apple, including the pips, then blow out the candle.

Unicorn Spell for Wealth

Unicorn spell for wealth

Return to your altar. Light a candle (silver or gold is a good colour for this purpose) and arrange everything how you like it. You will need to add a coin.

As you gaze into the flickering light of the candle, let your mind relax. Once again, with the guidance of the unicorn, ask your instincts and intuition to tell you all the things that for you mean wealth. This could mean independence, love, friendship, strength . . . Remember that wealth is not just about money – although that is important, too! The unicorn may make unexpected ideas and words pop into your head. Take notice of what it tells you.

List in your mind (or on paper) all of the material possessions that you own, or which you have the advantage of. For example, do you live in a house? Do you have access to a car? Maybe you own a musical instrument? Or a pet? Say 'Thank you', either in your mind or aloud, to the unicorn, for all the wealth that you already have, which you may actually find is considerable. List all of these things, and then add to the list some of the things that you might not yet have, but which you would like to own one day.

Blow out the candle, and put the coin in your pocket.

If you are good at keeping lists in your head, do so. If you're better at reflecting back on a paper list, write it all down. Check the list in a few weeks, and see if anything changes!

Unicorn Spell for a Little Magic Every Day

Unicorn spell for a little magic every day

Return to your altar. Light a candle (a rainbow-coloured one is good for this purpose, but not easy to get hold of. A lilac one will do just as well). Arrange everything in a way that suits you. You will need to add your favourite crystal or stone – one that holds meaning for you personally.

Gaze into the flickering light of the candle and let your mind relax. After a few minutes, lie down on the floor or on your bed, close your eyes, and ask the unicorn to take you into his magical kingdom. Go wherever he takes you; perhaps you'll see a castle with golden turrets, or a forest with a waterfall, or perhaps you'll see your own home from high up in the sky as you gallop through the clouds on your unicorn's back. Gradually bring yourself back into the 'real' world. Blow out the candle and put the crystal somewhere safe.

Draw what you saw, or write about it. Then ask the unicorn to help you notice something magical every day. This might be something very small, something that no one else has noticed, such as a beautiful feather or an unusual rock or cloud. Write down each magical event in a diary or notebook.

Unicorn Inspiration

Always be yourself,
UNLESS YOU CAN BE A
unicorn.
Then always be a
unicorn!

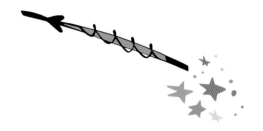

THOSE WHO DON'T
believe in magic
WILL NEVER FIND IT.

Sparkle
wherever you go!

Be a unicorn

IN A WORLD FULL OF

horses.

BEING A

buman

IS TOO COMPLICATED.

Time to be a

unicorn.

Be
magical!

Bibliography

American Museum of Natural History Staff. 'Unicorns, West and East'. American Museum of Natural History. Online at https://www.amnh.org/exhibitions/mythic-creatures/land-creatures-of-the-earth/unicorns-west-and-east/ (accessed 2 January 2018).

Ancient Origins Staff. 'The gentle and benevolent Qilin of Chinese mythology'. Ancient Origins: Reconstructing the Story of Humanity's Past. Online at http://www.ancient-origins.net/myths-legends/gentle-and-benevolent-qilin-chinese-mythology-001933 (accessed 2 January 2018).

Bennett, Clare. (12 January 2017.) 'Everything you ever wanted to know about unicorns but were afraid to ask'. *Tatler*. Online at http://www.tatler.com/article/facts-about-unicorns (accessed 2 January 2018).

Bressan, David. (22 September 2018.) 'Fossil legends – the mammoth as unicorn'. History of Geology. Online at http://historyofgeology.fieldofscience.com/2010/09/fossil-legends-mammoth-as-unicorn.html (accessed 2 January 2018).

Carroll, Lewis. *Through the Looking-Glass, and What Alice Found There*. Macmillan Publishers, 1871.

Dictionary.com Staff. 'Unicorn'. Dictionary.com Online at http://www.dictionary.com/browse/unicorn?s=t (accessed 2 January 2018).

Dream of Italy schedule of events. https://dreamofitaly.com/event/vinci-tuscany-unicorn-festival/ (accessed 2 January 2018).

Editors of the *Encyclopaedia Britannica*. 'Georges Cuvier, French zoologist'. *Encyclopaedia Britannica*. Online at https://www.britannica.com/biography/Georges-Cuvier (accessed 2 January 2018).

Editors of the *Encyclopaedia Britannica*. 'Otto von Guericke, Prussian physicist, engineer, and philosopher'. *Encyclopaedia Britannica*. Online at https://www.britannica.com/biography/Otto-von-Guericke (accessed 2 January 2018).

Editors of the *Encyclopaedia Britannica*. 'Qilin, Chinese mythology'. *Encyclopaedia Britannica*. Online at https://www.britannica.com/topic/qilin (accessed 2 January 2018).

Editors of the *Encyclopaedia Britannica*. 'Unicorn, mythological creature'. *Encyclopaedia Britannica*. Online at https://www.britannica.com/topic/unicorn (accessed 2 January 2018).

Editors at TSER. 'The Gender Unicorn'. Trans Student Educational Resources. Online at http://www.transstudent.org/what-we-do/graphics/gender-unicorn/ (accessed 2 January 2018).

Epsom Salt Council official website. www.epsomsaltcouncil.org (accessed 2 January 2018).

Fears, Danika. (2 March 2017.) 'That time Ringling Bros. claimed it had real unicorns'. The *New York Post*. Online at https://nypost.com/2017/03/02/how-unicorns-became-stars-of-the-greatest-show-on-earth/ (accessed 2 January 2018).

Festa dell' Unicorno official website. http://www.festaunicorno.com/ (accessed 2 January 2018).

Financial Times Staff. 'ft.com/lexicon: definition of unicorn'. The *Financial Times*. Online at http://lexicon.ft.com/Term?term=unicorn (accessed 2 January 2018).

Findley, James. (20 October 2016.) 'Unicorns in Shakespeare'. History Mash. Online at https://historymash.com/2016/10/20/unicorns-in-shakespeare/ (accessed 2 January 2018).

Fisher, Alice. (15 October 2017.) 'Why the unicorn has become the emblem for our times'. The *Guardian*. Online at https://www.theguardian.com/society/2017/oct/15/return-of-the-unicorn-the-magical-beast-of-our-times (accessed 2 January 2018).

Gregersen, Erik. 'Monoceros, astronomy'. *Encyclopaedia Britannica*. Online at https://www.britannica.com/place/Monoceros-astronomy (accessed 2 January 2018).

Grundhauser, Eric. (23 June 2015.) 'Unicorn horns and the Throne of Denmark'. Atlas Obscura, The Slate. Online at http://www.slate.com/blogs/atlas_obscura/2015/06/23/the_ceremonial_throne_of_denmark_passes_off_narwhal_tusk_as_unicorn_horn.html (accessed 2 January 2018).

Hovind, Eric. (19 July 2011.) 'Why does the Bible mention unicorns?' *Creation Today*. Online at http://creationtoday.org/why-does-the-bible-mention-unicorns/ (accessed 2 January 2018).

IMDb (Internet Movie Database). 'The Last Unicorn (1982)'. http://www.imdb.com/title/tt0084237/?ref_=nv_sr_1 (accessed 2 January 2018).

Johnstone, Lindsey. (6 May 2014.) 'Facts about Scotland's national animal the Unicorn'. The *Scotsman*. Online at https://www.scotsman.com/lifestyle/facts-about-scotland-s-national-animal-the-unicorn-1-3400212 (accessed 2 January 2018).

Keycraft Retail Insight Staff. (13 June 2017.) 'Why are unicorns so popular? And what does this mean for retail sales?' Keycraft Global. Online at http://www.keycraftglobal.com/news-and-insights/why-are-unicorns-so-popular/ (accessed 2 January 2018).

Lavers, Chris. *The Natural History of Unicorns*. Granta Books, London: 2010.

National Geographic Staff. 'Narwhal'. *National Geographic*. Online at https://www.nationalgeographic.com/animals/mammals/n/narwhal/ (accessed 2 January 2018).

Pai, Deanna. (20 April 2016.) 'The one thing you should always do before using a new skin care product'. *Glamour*. Online at https://www.glamour.com/story/the-right-way-to-test-a-new-skin-care-product (accessed 2 January 2018).

Quinn, Ben. (30 November 2012.) 'Unicorn lair "discovered" in North Korea.' The *Guardian*. Online at https://www.theguardian.com/world/2012/nov/30/unicorn-lair-discovered-north-korea (accessed 2 January 2018).

Quinn, Michelle. (16 March 2015.) 'Uber, Airbnb, Pinterest and the 30 other "unicorns" with all-male boards'. SiliconBeat, the tech blog of *The Mercury News*. Online at http://www.siliconbeat.com/2015/03/16/uber-airbnb-pinterest-and-the-30-other-unicorns-with-all-male-boards/?doing_wp_cron=1512137904.9270420074462890625000 (accessed 2 January 2018).

Sharples, Tiffany. (12 June 2008.) 'A brief history of the unicorn'. *Time* magazine. Online at http://content.time.com/time/health/article/0,8599,1814227,00.html (accessed 2 January 2018).

Souliere, Michelle. 'Dr. Dove's unicorn'. Strange Maine. Online at http://strangemaine. blogspot.co.uk/2006/03/dr-doves-unicorn.html (accessed 2 January 2018).

Suich, Alexandra. 'Year of the unicorn: Startups will need to prove their worth or face the cull'. *The Economist*. Online at http://www.theworldin.com/article/10454/year-unicorn?fsrc=scn/tw/te/bl/ed/theworldin2016 (accessed 2 January 2018).

Vettel, Phil. (18 October 1985.) 'Telling the living truth about the unicorn'. The *Chicago Tribune*. Online at http://articles.chicagotribune.com/1985-10-18/entertainment/8503110287_1_lancelot-ringling-brothers-animal (accessed 2 January 2018).

Acknowledgements

I would like to thank every person involved in the whirlwind of sparkles that was the creation of *Unicornucopia*. A big thank you to Laura Korzon for her whimsical illustrations of narwhals, unicorns, and all manner of magic. (With a particular shout-out for her narwhal cross-section!) Immense gratitude to the immeasurably talented Jacqui Caulton for her gorgeous design and unwavering professionalism. Thank you to the lovely Adele Nozedar for the excellent section on unicorn spells and charms. Thanks to the amazing Team Unicorn: Catherine, Dean, and Helena. Thank you to Oli M. for conjuring the initial idea and title. A heartfelt thank you to Eli Erlick at Transstudent.org for permission to use the Gender Unicorn, and to my sister Meghan for first bringing this concept to my attention. A very warm thank you to my mom and Aunt Marie for sharing the family pancake recipe, and to Rebecca for sharing her glorious rainbow cake recipe (and for first sharing the result at my daughter's weather-themed 1st birthday party). Thank you to Mary T., Hazel E., and Lucy V. for the unicorn enthusiasm.

About the author & illustrator

Caitlin Doyle is a writer, editor, and creative writing teacher, based in London, England. Caitlin has written and edited several books for adults and children for almost 20 years, including *Outrageously Adorable Dog Knits*, *Why I Love Bedtime*, and *Girls Can Do Anything* (also called *We Can Do Anything*). Her work ranges from children's picture books to adult reference, and everything in between.

Laura Korzon is an artist, illustrator, and designer, born and raised in Lancaster, Pennsylvania, U.S.A. She graduated from Rhode Island School of Design in 2010 and spends her days creating colourful graphics for cards, stationery, clothing, and more. *Unicornucopia* is her first book.